Christmas Songbook for Ukulele
Book with Audio Access

By
Bert Casey

For Soprano, Concert, & Tenor Ukuleles
C Tuning (G, C, E, A)

Free Online Audio Access
Go to this address on the internet:

http://cvls.com/extras/ukexmas/

Copyright 2018 by Watch & Learn, Inc./Bert Casey 1st Printing
ALL RIGHTS RESERVED. Any copying, arranging, or adapting of this work without the
consent of the owner is an infringement of copyright.

About This Book

This songbook features beginner to intermediate arrangements for classic Christmas songs. The first arrangement you will learn for each song features a melody line along with the chord progression and the strumming pattern for ukulele. The second arrangement displays each song along with chord progressions, lyrics, and vocal melody lines. This is a great setup for sing-alongs because the lyrics are written in a large font so that multiple singers and musicians can read along.

Audio Tracks

This course also includes access to audio tracks to help you learn and practice. We have included three different recordings of each song. The first version features just the ukulele playing the strumming pattern along with the chord progression and a click track. The second version has the ukulele playing along with other instruments. The last recording features the other instruments with no ukulele so that you can practice playing the ukulele part in context.

You may access these files by going to the following web address:

http://cvls.com/extras/ukexmas/

The Author

Bert Casey, the author of this book, has been a professional performer and teacher in the Atlanta area for over 30 years. Bert plays several instruments (acoustic guitar, electric guitar, bass guitar, mandolin, banjo, ukulele, and flute) and has written seven instructional courses (*Acoustic Guitar Primer, Acoustic Guitar Book 2, Electric Guitar Primer, Bass Guitar Primer, Mandolin Primer, Flatpicking Guitar Songs, Ukulele Primer, Ukulele Chord Book,* and *Bluegrass Fakebook*).

Bert performed for several years in Atlanta and the Southeast with his bands Home Remedy and Blue Moon. His talent and willingness to share have helped thousands of students learn and experience the joy of playing a musical instrument.

More Ukulele Books

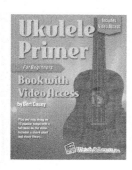

If you need to brush up on your technique or expand your song repertoire, try the *Ukulele Primer* by Bert Casey. It starts off with the absolute basics like tuning (G, C, E, A), left and right hand position, and how to strum. You'll learn chords and different strum patterns in the context of fifteen popular songs. It includes 90 minutes of online Video instruction. Entertain your friends and family by learning how to play this great instrument that is soaring in popularity.

The *Ukulele Chord Book* contains over 300 chords with photos to illustrate how to play each chord. The accompanying diagram displays proper fret position, fingering, and labels the notes of the chord. Shows 12 common chord types in two different neck positions in all twelve major keys. Also includes sections on Moveable Chords, Common Chords in Each Major Key, and a full neck diagram of the ukulele with all notes labeled. This handy book will help advance your ukulele playing to the next level.

Companion Christmas Books

These books contain the same songs and arrangements as the *Christmas Songbook for Ukulele*. Enjoy the Christmas season with your musical friends as they play and sing along with you.

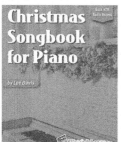

Each course contains three versions of the Audio Tracks (the instrument by itself, all of the instruments together, and just the other instruments so you can practice playing along in context).

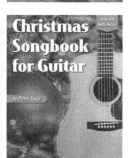

These books are available at Amazon.com.

Table Of Contents

                                                                           Page

Section 1 - Getting Started

- The Ukulele 7
- Parts of the Ukulele 8
- Tuning 9
- Holding the Ukulele 10
- Left Hand Position 11
- Strumming 12
- Ukulele Notation 13

Section 2 - Christmas Songs

- Chords, Strums, & Fingerpicking 15
- Silent Night 16
- Silent Night - Fingerpicking 17
- Auld Lang Syne 18-19
- Jingle Bells 20-21
- What Child is This 22-23
- We Wish You a Merry Christmas 24-25
- Joy to the World 26-27
- The First Noel 28-29
- Deck the Hall 30-31
- O Christmas Tree 32-33
- We Three Kings 34-35
- God Rest Ye Merry Gentlemen 36-37
- Hark! The Herald Angels Sing 38-39

                                                              Page
Section 3 - Lyrics
    Auld Lang Syne 41

    Deck the Hall 42

    God Rest Ye Merry Gentlemen 43

    Hark! The Herald Angels Sing 44

    Jingle Bells 45

    Joy to the World 46

    O Christmas Tree 47

    Silent Night 48

    The First Noel 49

    We Three Kings 50

    We Wish You a Merry Christmas 51

    What Child is This 52

Appendix
    Chord Chart 54-55

Section 1
Getting Started

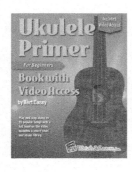

We are including the Getting Started Section from the *Ukulele Primer* course in case you need to brush up on your technique. If you find some of these songs and techniques too difficult, this is a great refresher course and is available on Amazon.com.

The Ukulele

There are four main types of ukuleles as shown by the photos below. This course will work with the Soprano, Concert, and Tenor ukes, all tuned G C E A.

The baritone ukulele is usually tuned like the first four strings of a guitar (D G B E) and will not be used in this course. I'll be using a tenor ukulele primarily, but you could use a soprano or concert uke with this course.

Soprano   Concert   Tenor   Baritone

Take your ukulele to your local music store to make sure it is in good playing condition and has good strings. If it needs any repairs, they can probably do it on the spot.

Get to know the folks at your local music store. They can be a great help with supplies, lessons, & advice.

Parts of the Ukulele

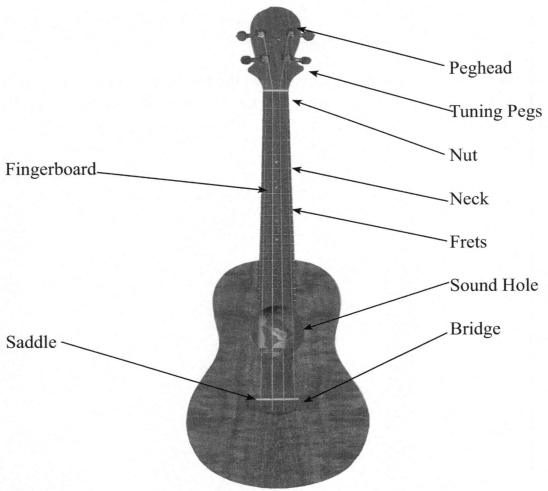

If you need to buy a ukulele, it is usually safer to purchase your first instrument from a reputable music store, who will make sure that the instrument is adjusted properly and offer service after the sale. Resist the temptation to buy a cheap plastic uke. These are little more than toys and can be very hard to play. You should purchase a case for your ukulele because many are broken by accident. There are several types of cases to pick from. You may buy a hard shell, which is most durable, a soft shell, or a gig bag. A case should keep the ukulele dry and protected when being transported.

Your ukulele should be stored in a neutral environment. This means not too cold, not too hot, not too wet, and not too dry. The wood in a ukulele is subject to change and will expand or contract in response to its environment. Too much of any of these conditions could cause permanent damage. For example, never leave your uke in your car for long periods of time during summer or winter months. Attics and basements tend to be poor locations for storing a ukulele as well.

 *Always use a case or gig bag when transporting your instrument from one place to another.*

Tuning

There are several popular tunings for the ukulele. The two most common are the C tuning (G, C, E, A) and the A tuning (A, D, F#, B) with the C tuning being the most popular.

This course will use a soprano, concert, or tenor ukulele tuned to a C tuning (G C E A). Tune the four strings of the ukulele to the same pitch as the four notes shown on the piano in the following diagrams.

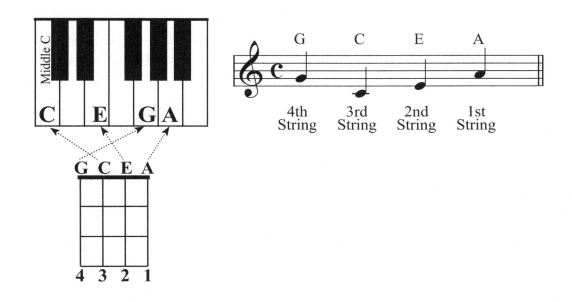

Electronic Tuner

An electronic tuner is the fastest and most accurate way to tune a ukulele. I highly recommend getting one. It may take months or years for a beginner to develop the skills to tune a uke correctly by ear. The electronic tuner is more precise and is used by virtually every professional player.

TIP: Never leave your instrument in a car or trunk during extreme heat or cold.

Holding the Ukulele

Many ukulele players are self taught and have developed their own unique style and methods of playing. There is no one correct way to play the uke. I'll be showing you the most common techniques to use and the ones that I use.

At first you will be holding the ukulele sitting down. Use a straight back chair or stool so you can sit with good posture and have free arm movement without banging the uke on your arms or the furniture.

Sit erect with both feet on the floor. The ukulele should be braced against your chest with your right forearm so the neck doesn't move when you change hand positions. Press lightly with the right forearm to press the uke against your ribs. The left hand is used for balance.

The standing position is harder and takes a little more getting used to. Again, press the uke against your right side with your right forearm. You can use a ukulele strap if you like.

Always keep an extra set of strings in your case. You never know when you will break one.

Left Hand Position

Arm Position

The left elbow should hang freely to the outside of the left leg. Make sure you aren't resting the left elbow on your leg. This will avoid undue stress on the elbow and wrist.

Thumb Position

You will see different players use different thumb positions, but I prefer this position because it allows you to play all of the chords without having to change your thumb position (Figure A).

The pad of your left thumb should be positioned on the center of the back of the ukulele neck. This will be our core position (Figure B).

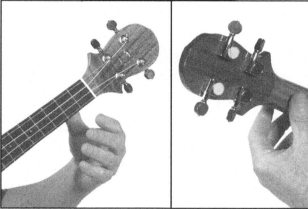

Figure A **Figure B**

Wrist Position

The wrist should be below the ukulele neck in a comfortable position. Don't strain your wrist to one side or the other (Figure C).

Figure C

Fingernails

You will need to keep your fingernails trimmed so that you can easily press down on the fingerboard.

Don't store your ukulele in the attic or basement. Extreme dryness or dampness can be bad.

Strumming

There are a variety of ways to strum the ukulele. You can use your thumb, your index finger, a felt pick, or fingerpick. I'll use the index finger for this course.

Thumb   **Index Finger**   **Felt Pick**

Index Finger Strum

Curl your right index (Figure 1). Place the thumb on the side of the first joint of the index finger (Figure 2). Strike the strings with the finger nail of your right index finger (Figure 3).

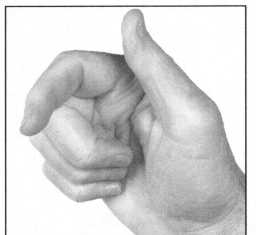  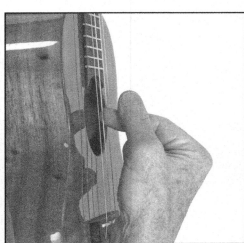

Figure 1   **Figure 2**   **Figure 3**

Right Hand Position

Position your right hand so that you strike the strings in the center of the sound hole. Don't brace your right hand on the ukulele. It should move freely with no part of the hand or wrist touching the ukulele. You should be moving from your wrist and not the elbow.

 Practicing a little each day is better than practicing a lot all at once.

Ukulele Notation

The ukulele notation in this book is written on two lines or staves. The top staff is the melody line with lyrics. The bottom line is the strumming pattern for the right hand.

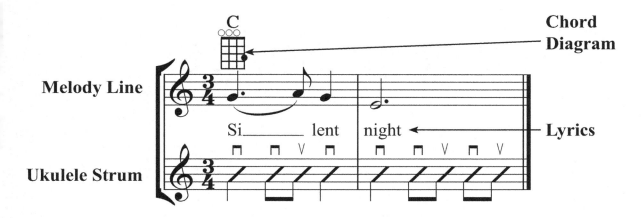

The exercises contain only one line or staff. This is the ukulele strumming notation.

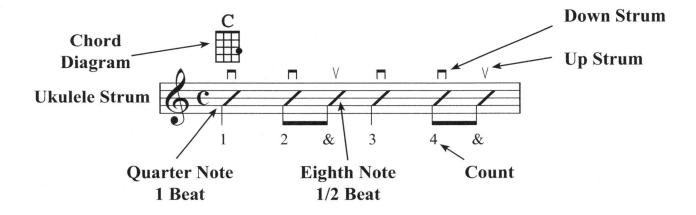

Practice new songs slowly and relaxed. Work on speed after you can play it perfectly.

Section 2
Christmas Songs

Chords, Strums, & Fingerpicking 15
Silent Night 16
Silent Night - Fingerpicking 17
Auld Lang Syne 18-19
Jingle Bells 20-21
What Child is This 22-23
We Wish You a Merry Christmas 24-25
Joy to the World 26-27
The First Noel 28-29
Deck the Hall 30-31
O Christmas Tree 32-33
We Three Kings 34-35
God Rest Ye Merry Gentlemen 36-37
Hark! The Herald Angels Sing 38-39

Online Audio Access is available at this address on the internet:

http://cvls.com/extras/ukexmas/

Chord Diagrams

The first song is a three chord song in the key of C and we'll use the C, F, & G chords.

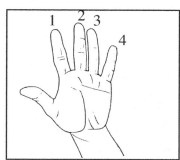

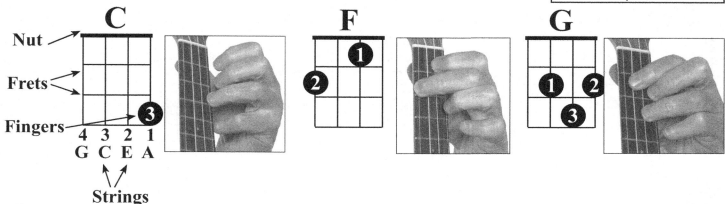

Strum Exercise

The first song is in 3/4 time, which means there are 3 beats per measure and we count 1 2 3, 1 2 3. The strum will be down down up down, down down up down and will be counted 1 2 & 3, 1 2 & 3. See page 7 for more detail on strumming notation.

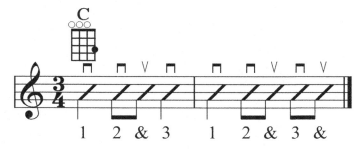

Fingerpicking Pattern

On page 11, we'll also play *Silent Night* using a fingerpicking pattern. The right thumb will play the 3rd and 4th string, the right index finger will play the 2nd string, and the right middle finger will play the first string. See page 7 for more detail on fingerpicking tablature.

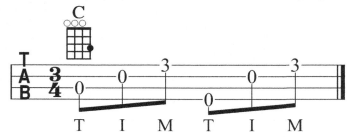

Silent Night

Silent Night - Fingerpicking

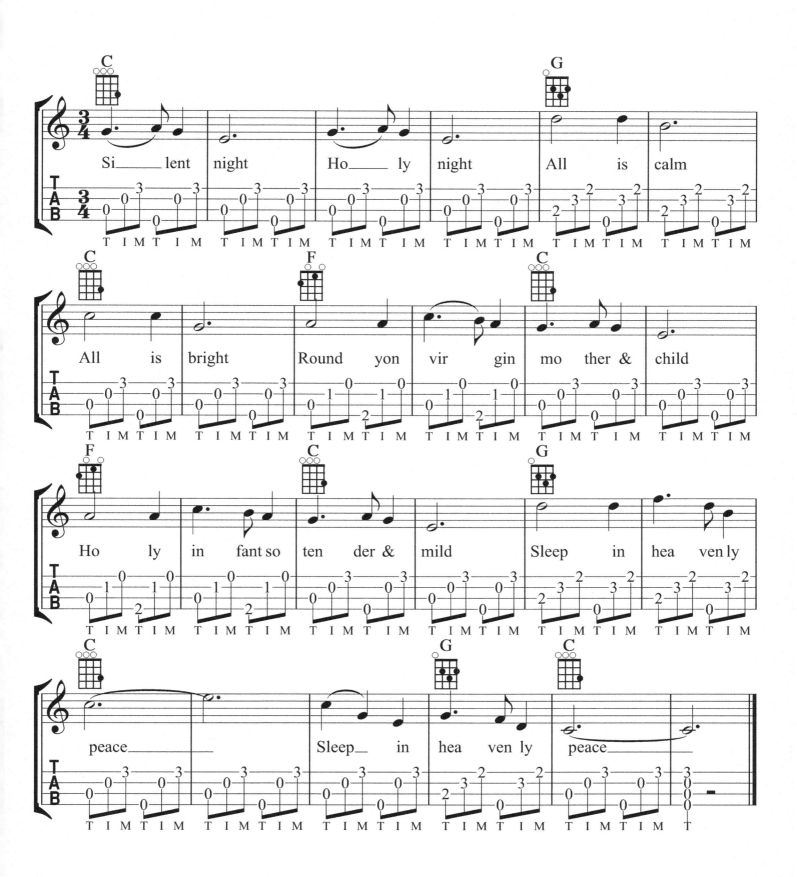

Chords

Auld Lang Syne is a three chord song in the key of G, so we'll use the G, C, & D chords. There are several ways to finger the D chord depending on your fingers size and dexterity.

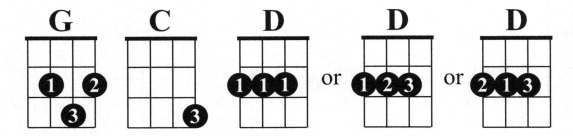

Strum Pattern

This song is in 4/4 time which means there are four beats per measure and we count 1 2 3 4, 1 2 3 4. The strum pattern will be down down up down down up and is counted:

1 2 & 3 4 & 1 2 & 3 4 &.

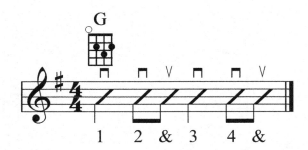

Auld Lang Syne is sung at the stroke of midnight on New Year's Eve.

Auld Lang Syne

Chords

Jingle Bells is a four chord song in the key of F using the F, B♭, C, & G chords.

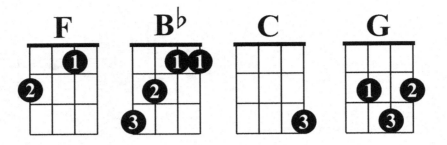

Strum Pattern

This song is in 4/4 time and the strum will be down down down down up and is counted:

1 2 3 4 & 1 2 3 4 &.

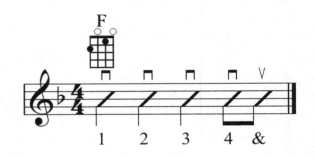

Jingle Bells

Chords

Four new chords in this song: B, Am, Em, and Bm

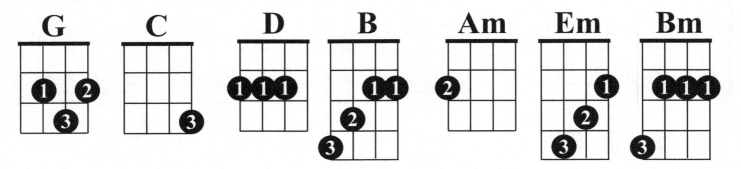

Strum Pattern

3/4 time again. This is the same strum used in *Silent Night* and is counted:

1 2 & 3 1 2 & 3 4 &.

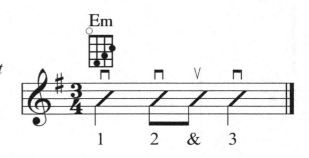

What Child is This

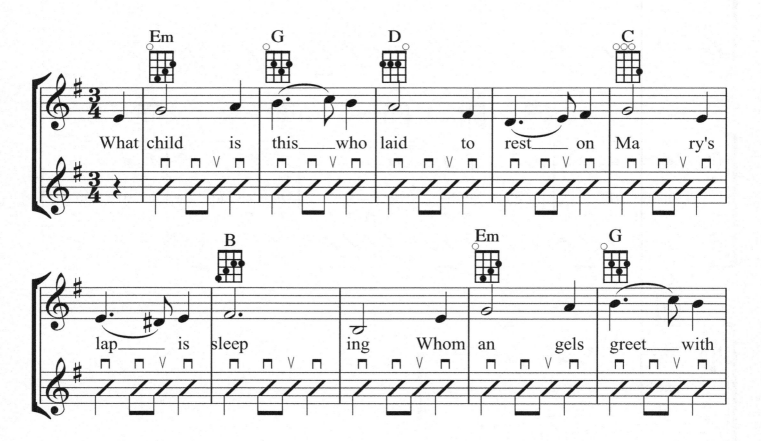

What child is this____who laid to rest____ on Ma ry's lap____ is sleep ing Whom an gels greet____with

22

Chords

We'll add an A chord for this song, and some faster switching between the chords.

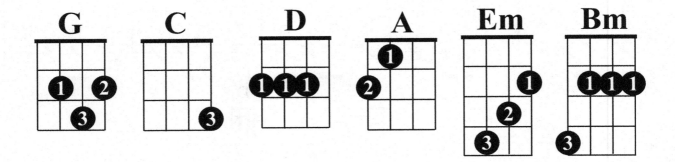

Strum Pattern

3/4 time again and we'll use a two measure strum.

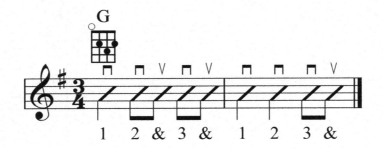

We Wish You a Merry Christmas

Traditional

Chords

We'll use the D, G, & A chords again.

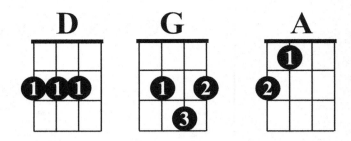

Strum Pattern

We'll use different combinations of this two measure strum in this tune. This is a pretty fast tempo with some quick chord changes.

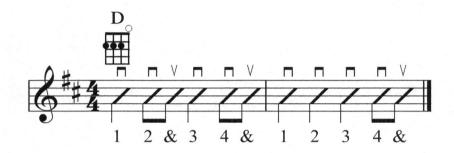

Joy to the World

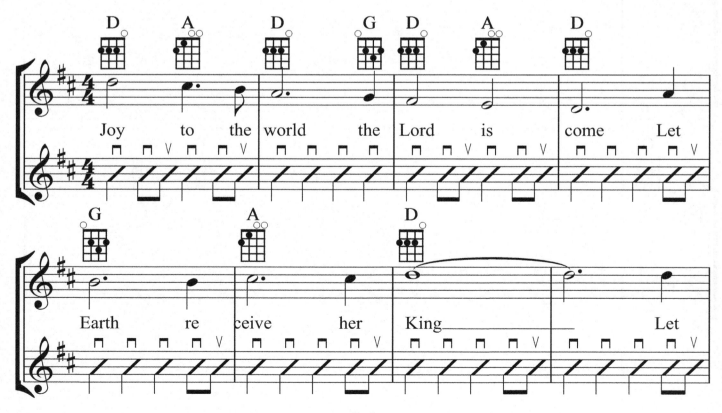

26

Chords

We'll use the D, G, A, and Bm chords again for this tune.

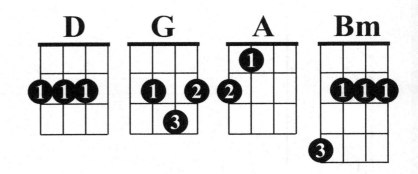

Strum Pattern

This is second measure of the two measure strum that we used in *We Wish You A Merry Christmas*.

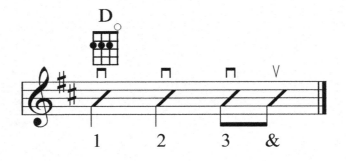

The First Noel

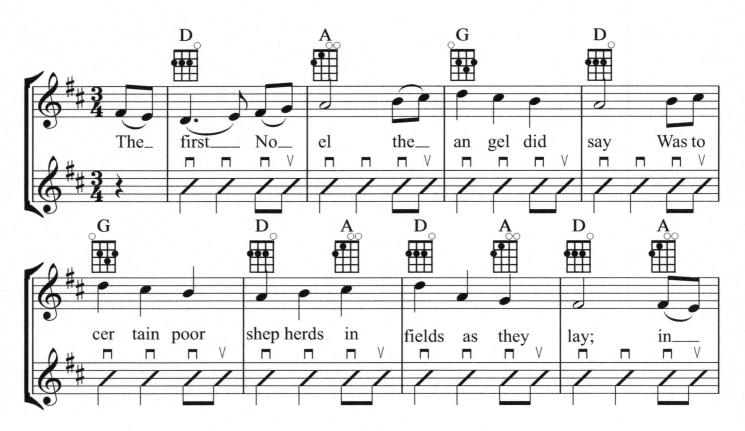

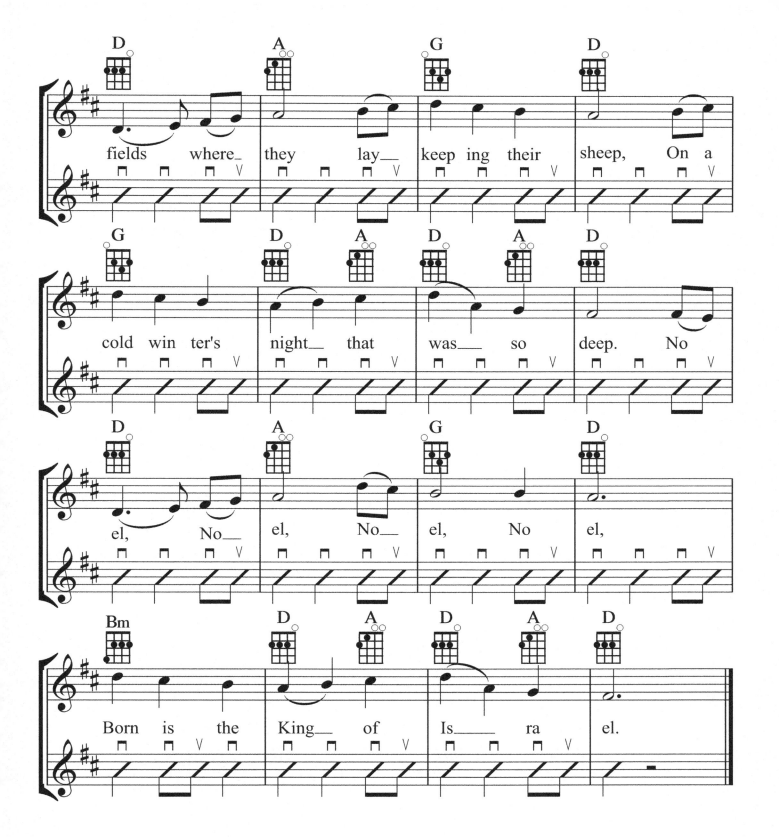

Chords

Let's add the G⁷ and Dm⁷ chords to our repertoire.

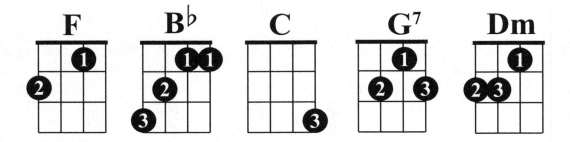

Strum Pattern

We'll use two different strums in this song. The first one we've used before. The second strum follows the rhythm of the melody in the Fa la la la la part.

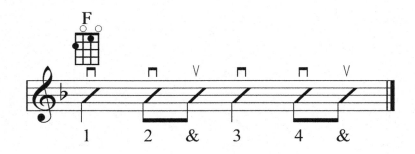

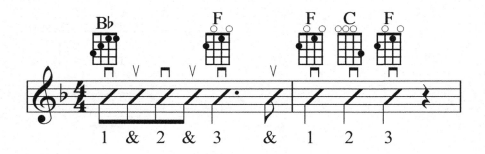

Deck the Hall

Chords

Let's learn the C⁷ and Gm⁷ chords for this tune.

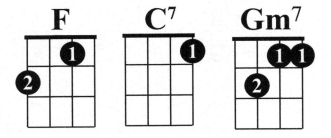

Strum Pattern

Back to 3/4 or waltz time for this song and the strum will be a little different. Once again, we'll be following the rhythm of the melody with the strumming pattern.

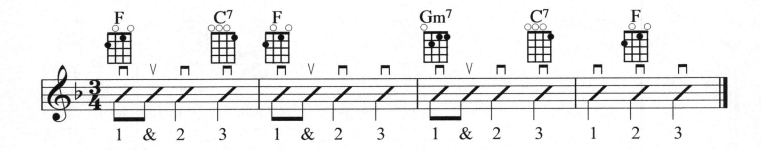

O Christmas Tree

Chords

These are all chords that we've already used, but we'll use a different fingering for the C chord. It's the same as the B chord, but moved up one fret to the 3rd fret.

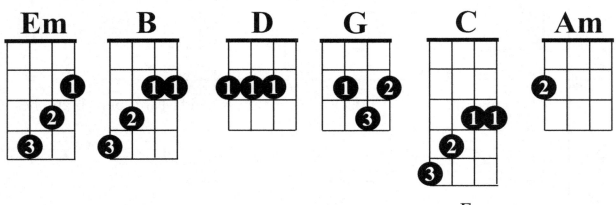

Strum Pattern

You should be familiar with this strum pattern by now as we've used it in several songs.

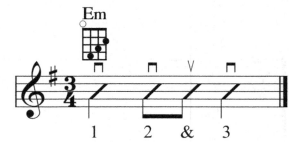

We Three Kings

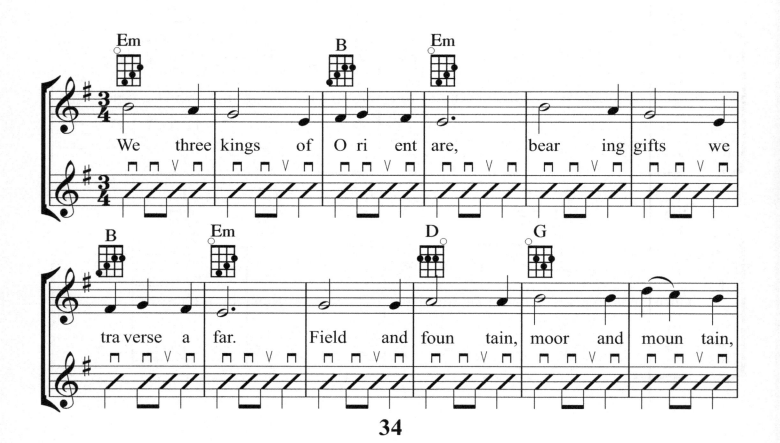

Chords

We have used all of these chords before, but there are some quick changes again.

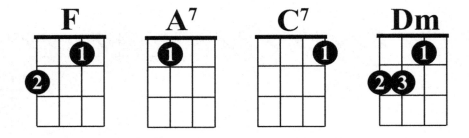

Strum Pattern

You should be familiar with this strum pattern by now as we've used it in several songs.

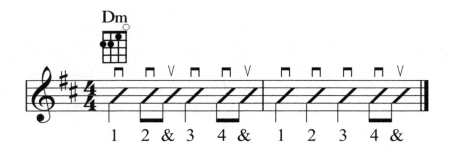

God Rest Ye Merry Gentlemen

Chords

E^7 is the new chord for this song.

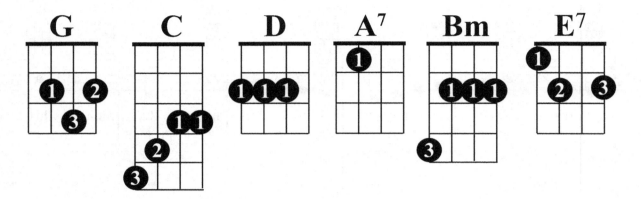

Strum Pattern

Here's a familiar strum pattern that we've used several times before.

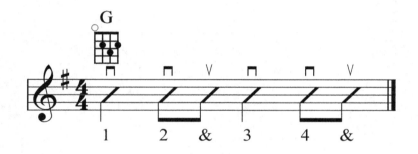

Hark! The Herald Angels Sing

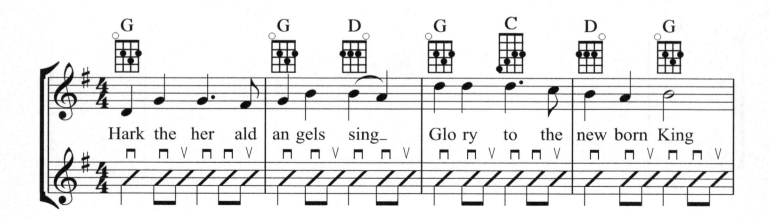

38

Lyrics

Auld Lang Syne 41
Deck the Hall 42
God Rest Ye Merry Gentlemen 43
Hark! The Herald Angels Sing 44
Jingle Bells 45
Joy to the World 46
O Christmas Tree 47
Silent Night 48
The First Noel 49
We Three Kings 50
We Wish You a Merry Christmas 51
What Child is This 52

This section contains the melody line, lyrics, and chord progressions so that you can play the complete version of the songs with all of the lyrics. This also works great for jam sessions or playing on stage because the lyrics are in a large font with the chord progression on each verse.

Auld Lang Syne

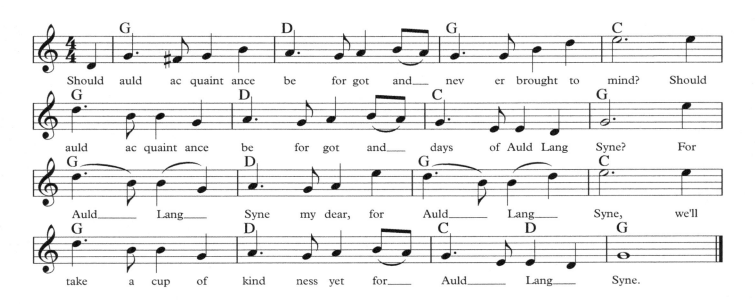

Should auld acquaintance be forgot
 G   D
And never brought to mind
 G   C
Should auld acquaintance be forgot
 G   D
And days of Auld Lang Syne
 C   D   G
For Auld Lang Syne my dear
 G   D
For Auld Lang Syne
 G   C
We'll take a cup of kindness yet
 G   D
For Auld Lang Syne
 C   D   G

Note - There are other verses to *Auld Lang Syne*, but it's typically performed with only this verse at the stroke of midnight on New Year's Eve. It's an old Scottish tune and is translated as "old long time". You'll also hear singers substitute old for Auld in the first two lines.

Deck the Hall

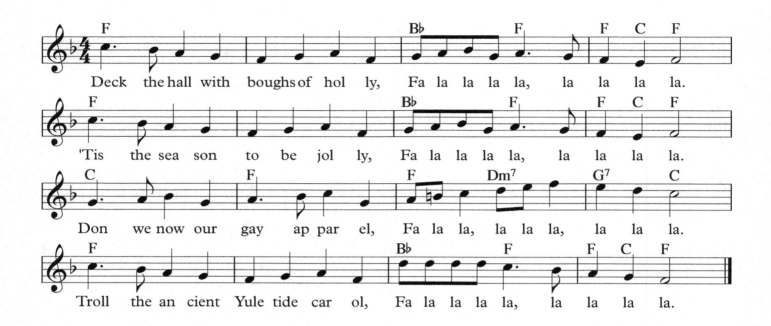

Deck the hall with boughs of holly
Fa la la la la, la la la la
'Tis the season to be jolly
Fa la la la la, la la la la
Don we now our gay apparel
Fa la la, la la la, la la la
Troll the ancient yuletide carol
Fa la la la la, la la la la

See the blazing yule before us
Fa la la la la, la la la la
Strike the harp and join the chorus
Fa la la la la, la la la la
Follow me in merry measure
Fa la la, la la la, la la la
While I tell of yule tide treasure
Fa la la la la, la la la la

Fast away the old year passes
Fa la la la la, la la la la
Hail the new year lads and lases
Fa la la la la, la la la la
Sing we joyous all together
Fa la la, la la la, la la la
Heedless of the wind and weather
Fa la la la la, la la la la

God Rest Ye Merry Gentlemen

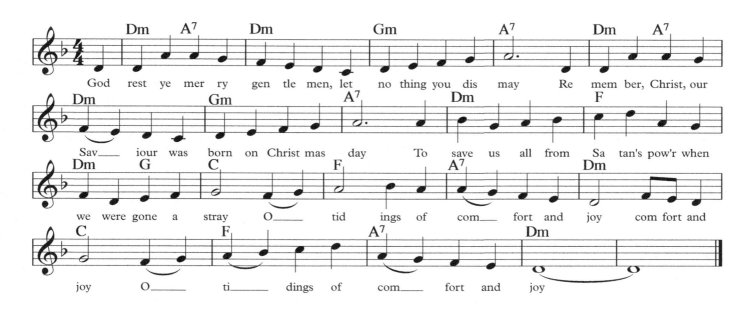

God rest ye merry gentlemen, let nothing you dismay
  Dm   A⁷   Dm   Gm   A⁷
Remember Christ, our Saviour, was born on Christmas day
  Dm   F   Dm   G   C
To save us all from Satan's pow'r when we were gone astray
 F   A⁷   .Dm   C
O tidings of comfort and joy, comfort and joy
 F   A⁷   .Dm
O tidings of comfort and joy

(Chords: Dm A⁷ Dm Gm A⁷ / Dm A⁷ Dm Gm A⁷ / Dm F Dm G C / F A⁷ Dm C / F A⁷ Dm)

In Bethlehem, in Israel, this blessed Babe was born
And laid within a manger upon this blessed morn
That which His Mother Mary did nothing take in scorn
O tidings of comfort and joy, comfort and joy
O tidings of comfort and joy

From God our Heavenly Father a blessed angel came
And unto certain shepherds brought tiding to the same
How that in Bethlehem was born the Son of God by name
O tidings of comfort and joy, comfort and joy
O tidings of comfort and joy

Hark! The Herald Angels Sing

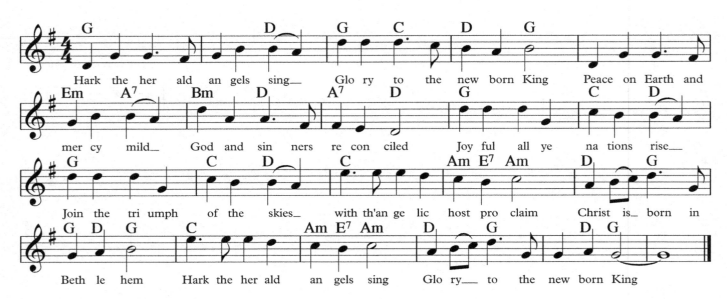

    G   D   G   C   D   G
Hark the herald angels sing Glory to the newborn King
 G   Em A⁷ Bm   D.   A⁷   D
Peace on Earth and mercy mild God and sinners reconciled
 G   C   D   G   C   D
Joyful all ye nations rise, join the triumph of the skies
 C   Am E⁷ Am   D   G   D G
With th'angelic host proclaim, Christ is born in Bethlehem
 C   Am E⁷ Am   D   G   D G
Hark the herald angels sing, Glory to the newborn King

    G   D   G   C   D   G
Christ by highest heav'n adored Christ, the everlasting Lord!
 G   Em A⁷ Bm   D   A⁷   D
Late in time behold Him come offspring of the virgin's womb
 G   C   D   G   C D
Veiled in flesh the Godhead see, hail the'incarnate Deity
 C   Am E⁷ Am   D   G   D G
Pleased as man with man to dwell, Jesus our Immanuel
 C   Am E⁷ Am   D   G   D G
Hark the herald angels sing, Glory to the newborn King

    G   D   G   C   D   G
Hail, the heav'n born Prince of Peace, hail the Son of righteousness
 G   Em   A⁷   Bm   D   A⁷   D
Light and life to all He brings, ris'n with healing in His wings
 G   C   D G   C   D
Mild He lays His glory by, born that man no more may die
 C   Am   E⁷ Am   D   G.   D   G.
Born to raise the sons of earth, born to give them second birth
 C   Am E⁷ Am   D   G   D G
Hark the herald angels sing, Glory to the newborn King

Jingle Bells

Dashing through the snow in a one horse open sleigh
O'er the fields we go laughing all the way
Bells on bobtail ring making spirits bright
What fun it is to ride and sing a sleighing song tonight Oh

Chorus
Jingle bells, jingle bells, jingle all the way
Oh what fun it is to ride in a one horse open sleigh, hey
Jingle bells, jingle bells, jingle all the way
Oh what fun it is to ride in a one horse open sleigh

A day or two ago I thought I'd take a ride
And soon Miss Fanny Bright was seated at my side
The horse was lean and lank, misfortune seemed his lot
We got into a drifted bank and then we go upsot Oh
Chorus

Joy to the World

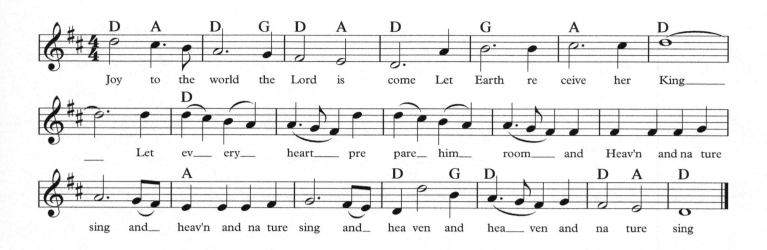

Joy to the world the Lord is come Let Earth re ceive her King
Let ev ery heart pre pare him room and Heav'n and na ture
sing and heav'n and na ture sing and hea ven and hea ven and na ture sing

    D A   D   G   D   A D
Joy to the world! The Lord is come
     G   A   D
Let earth receive her King
    D
Let every heart prepare Him room
And Heav'n and nature sing
     A
And Heav'n and nature sing
    D   G D   A D
And Heav'n and Heav'n and nature sing

  D A   D   G D A D
Joy to the world! The Savior reigns
    G   A   D
Let men their songs employ
       D
While fields and floods, rocks, hills, and plains
Repeat the sounding joy
      A
Repeat the sounding joy
   D G D   A D
Repeat, repeat the sounding joy

 D A   D   G   D A D
He rules the world with truth and grace
     G   A   D
And makes the nations prove
    D
The glories of His righteousness
And wonders of His love
     A
And wonders of His love
    D   G   D   A D
And wonders and wonders of His love

O Christmas Tree

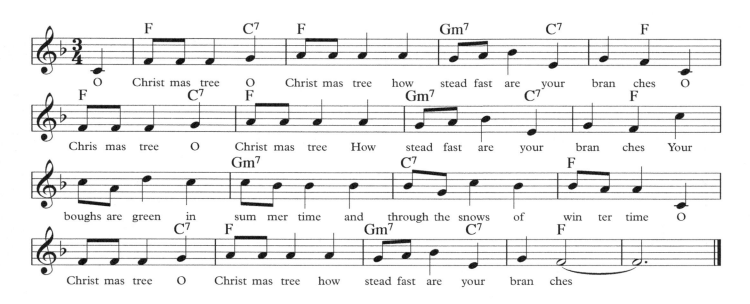

O <u>F</u>Christmas tree, <u>C7</u>O <u>F</u>Christmas tree, how <u>Gm7</u>stead fast are <u>C7</u>your <u>F</u>branches
O <u>F</u>Christmas tree, <u>C7</u>O <u>F</u>Christmas tree, how <u>Gm7</u>stead fast are <u>C7</u>your <u>F</u>branches
You boughs are green in <u>Gm7</u>summer time and <u>C7</u>through the snows of <u>F</u>winter time
O <u>F</u>Christmas tree, <u>C7</u>O <u>F</u>Christmas tree, how <u>Gm7</u>stead fast are <u>C7</u>your <u>F</u>branches

O <u>F</u>Christmas tree, <u>C7</u>O <u>F</u>Christmas tree, much <u>Gm7</u>pleasure doth <u>C7</u>thou bring <u>F</u>me
O <u>F</u>Christmas tree, <u>C7</u>O <u>F</u>Christmas tree, much <u>Gm7</u>pleasure doth <u>C7</u>thou bring <u>F</u>me
For every year the <u>Gm7</u>Christmas tree <u>C7</u>bring to us all both joy and glee <u>F</u>
O <u>F</u>Christmas tree, <u>C7</u>O <u>F</u>Christmas tree, much <u>Gm7</u>pleasure doth <u>C7</u>thou bring <u>F</u>me

O <u>F</u>Christmas tree, <u>C7</u>O <u>F</u>Christmas tree, thou <u>Gm7</u>candles shine <u>C7</u>out <u>F</u>brightly
O <u>F</u>Christmas tree, <u>C7</u>O <u>F</u>Christmas tree, thou <u>Gm7</u>candles shine <u>C7</u>out <u>F</u>brightly
Each bough doth hold its tiny <u>Gm7</u>light that <u>C7</u>makes each toy to <u>F</u>sparkle bright
O <u>F</u>Christmas tree, <u>C7</u>O <u>F</u>Christmas tree, thou <u>Gm7</u>candles shine <u>C7</u>out <u>F</u>brightly

Silent Night

Silent night, Holy night
All is calm, all is bright
Round yon virgin Mother and Child
Holy infant so tender and mild
Sleep in heavenly peace
Sleep in heavenly peace

Silent night, Holy night
Shepherds quake at the sight
Glories stream from heaven afar
Heav'nly hosts sing Alleluia
Christ the Savior is born!
Christ the Savior is born!

Silent night, Holy night
Son of God, love's pure light
Radiant beams from Thy holy face
With the dawn of redeeming grace
Jesus, Lord, at Thy birth
Jesus, Lord, at Thy birth

The First Noel

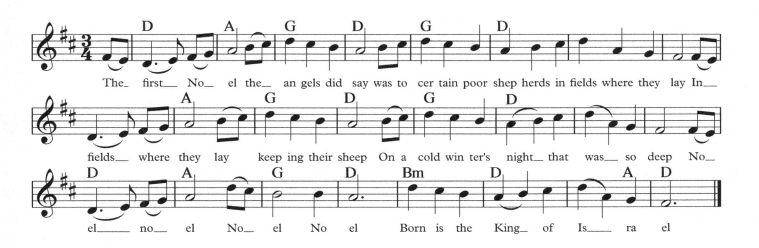

The first Noel the angels did say
Was to certain poor shepherds in fields where they lay
In fields where they lay keeping their sheep
On a cold winter's night that was so deep
Noel, Noel, Noel, Noel
Born is the King of Israel

They looked up and saw a star
Shining in the east, beyond them far
And to the earth it gave great light
And so it continued both day and night
Noel, Noel, Noel, Noel
Born is the King of Israel

We Three Kings

Chorus

Em   B7   Em
We three kings of Orient are
              B7   Em
Bearing gifts we traverse a far
Em   D   G
Field and fountain, moor and mountain
Am   B7   Em
Following yonder star
D   G   C   G
O, Star of wonder star of night
              C   G
Star of royal beauty bright
Em   D   C   D
Westward leading still proceeding
G   Em   C   G
Guide us to Thy perfect light

Em   B7   Em
Born a king on Bethlehem's plain
              B7   Em
Gold I bring to crown him again
Em   D   G
King forever, ceasing never
Am   B7   Em
Over us all to reign

Chorus

Em   B7   Em
Frankincense to offer have I
              B7   Em
Incense owns a Diety nigh
Em   D   G
Prayer and praising, voices raising
Am   B7   Em
Worshipping God on high

Chorus

We Wish You a Merry Christmas

Chorus

We ^Gwish you a merry ^CChristmas
We ^Awish you a merry ^DChristmas
We ^{Bm}wish you a merry ^{Em}Christmas
And a ^{Am}Happy ^DNew ^GYear
Good ^Gtidings we ^Dbring to ^Cyou and your ^GKing
Good tiding for ^DChristmas and a ^{Am}Happy ^DNew ^GYear

We ^Gall want some figgy ^Cpudding
We ^Aall want some figgy ^Dpudding
We ^{Bm}all want some figgy ^{Em}pudding
And a ^{Am}cup of ^Dgood ^Gcheer
Chorus

We ^Gwon't go until we ^Cget some
We ^Awon't go until we ^Dget some
We ^{Bm}won't go until we ^{Em}get some
So ^{Am}bring some ^Dright ^Ghere
Chorus

51

What Child is This

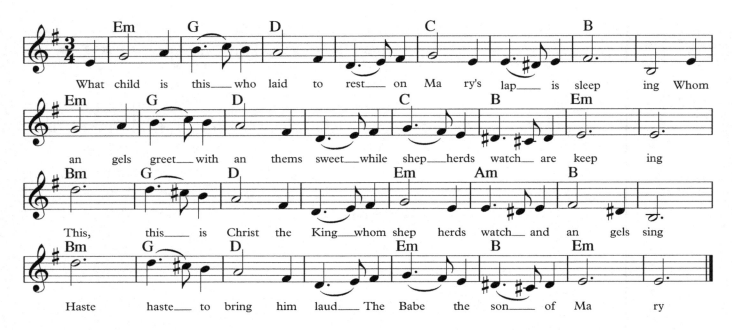

What child is this who laid to rest
   Em   G   D
On Mary's lap is sleeping
  C   B
Whom angels greet with anthems sweet
     Em   G   D
While shepherds watch are keeping
  C   B   Em
This, this is Christ the King
Bm G   D
Whom shepherds watch and angels sing
    Em   Am   B
Haste, haste to bring him laud
Bm G   D
The Babe, the son of Mary
  Em   B   Em

So bring him incense, gold, and myrrh
   Em   G   D
Come, peasant, king to own Him
     C   B
The King of Kings salvation brings
  Em   G   D
Let loving hearts enthrone Him
  C   B   Em
Raise, raise the song on high
Em G   D
The virgin sings her lullaby
   C   B
Joy, joy, for Christ, is born
Em G   D
The Babe the son of Mary
  C   B   Em

Appendix

Chord Chart

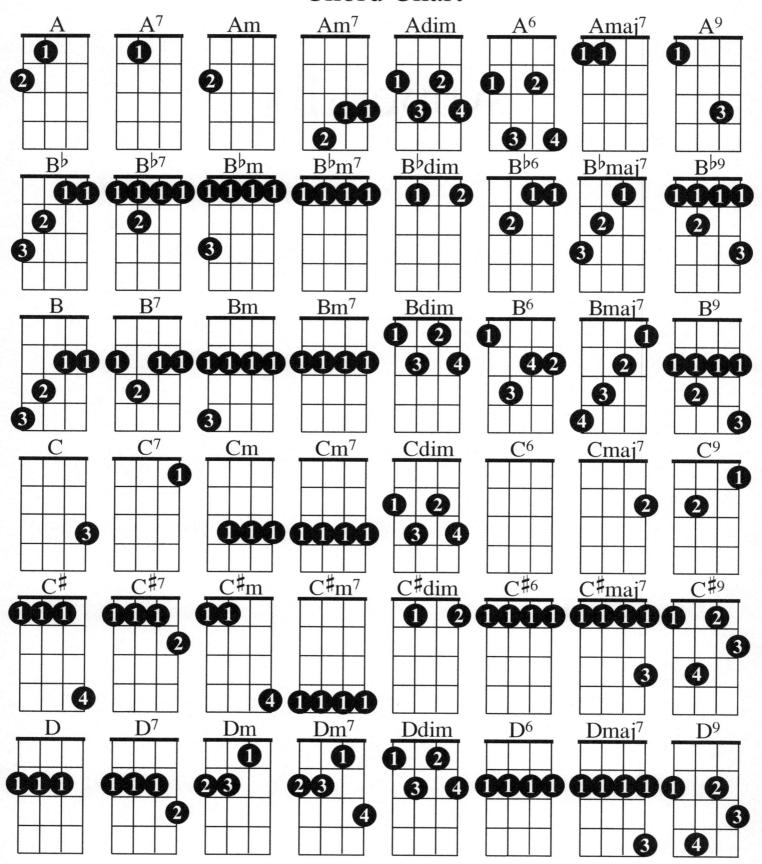

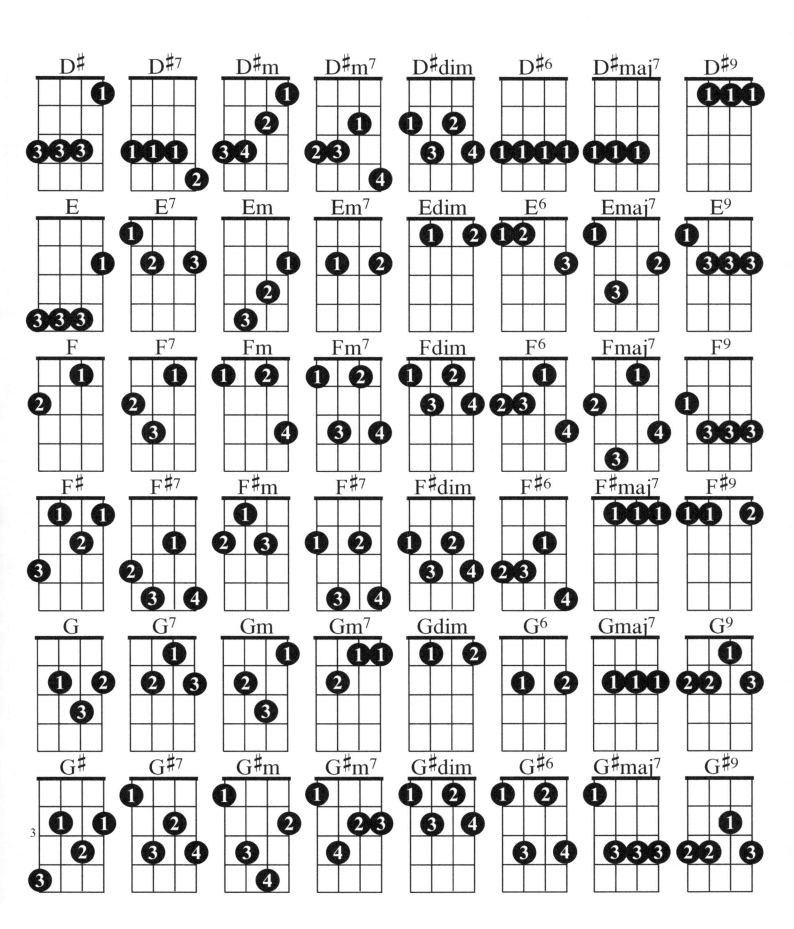

Made in the USA
Monee, IL
26 November 2019